HUMAN HABITATS

SKIN

By
Robin Twiddy

Enslow PUBLISHING

Published in 2022 by Enslow Publishing, LLC
101 W. 23rd Street, Suite 240,
New York, NY 10011

Cataloging-in-Publication Data

Names: Twiddy, Robin.
Title: Skin / Robin Twiddy.
Description: New York : Enslow Publishing, 2022. | Series: Human habitats | Includes glossary and index.
Identifiers: ISBN 9781978523722 (pbk.) | ISBN 9781978523746 (library bound) | ISBN 9781978523739 (6 pack) | ISBN 9781978523753 (ebook)
Subjects: LCSH: Skin--Juvenile literature. | Human physiology--Juvenile literature.
Classification: LCC QM484.T95 2022 | DDC 612.7'9--dc23

Designer: Gareth Liddington
Editor: John Wood

Printed in the United States of America

CPSIA compliance information: Batch #CS22ENS: For further information contact Enslow Publishing, New York, New York at 1-800-542-2595

TRICKY WORDS

Bacterium = singular (one bacterium)
Bacteria = plural (many bacteria)
Bacterial = to do with a bacterium or many bacteria

Fungus = singular (one fungus)
Fungi = plural (many fungi)
Fungal = to do with a fungus or many fungi

Photo credits:

4- ONYXprj, Fun way illustration, 6 - Alona Syplyak, Roi and Roi 8 - SaimonTraur, Maquiladora, Potapov Alexander, 14 - logistock, 16 - Thumbelina

Images are courtesy of Shutterstock.com. With thanks to Getty Images, Thinkstock Photo, and iStockphoto.

CONTENTS

Words that look like this can be found in the glossary on page 24.

WELCOME TO THE HUMAN HABITAT

Hi! I'm Mini Ventura. My cameraman, Dave, and I have been shrunk down so we can make a nature documentary all about the tiny things living in and on us. Follow us into the human habitat — a world within a world.

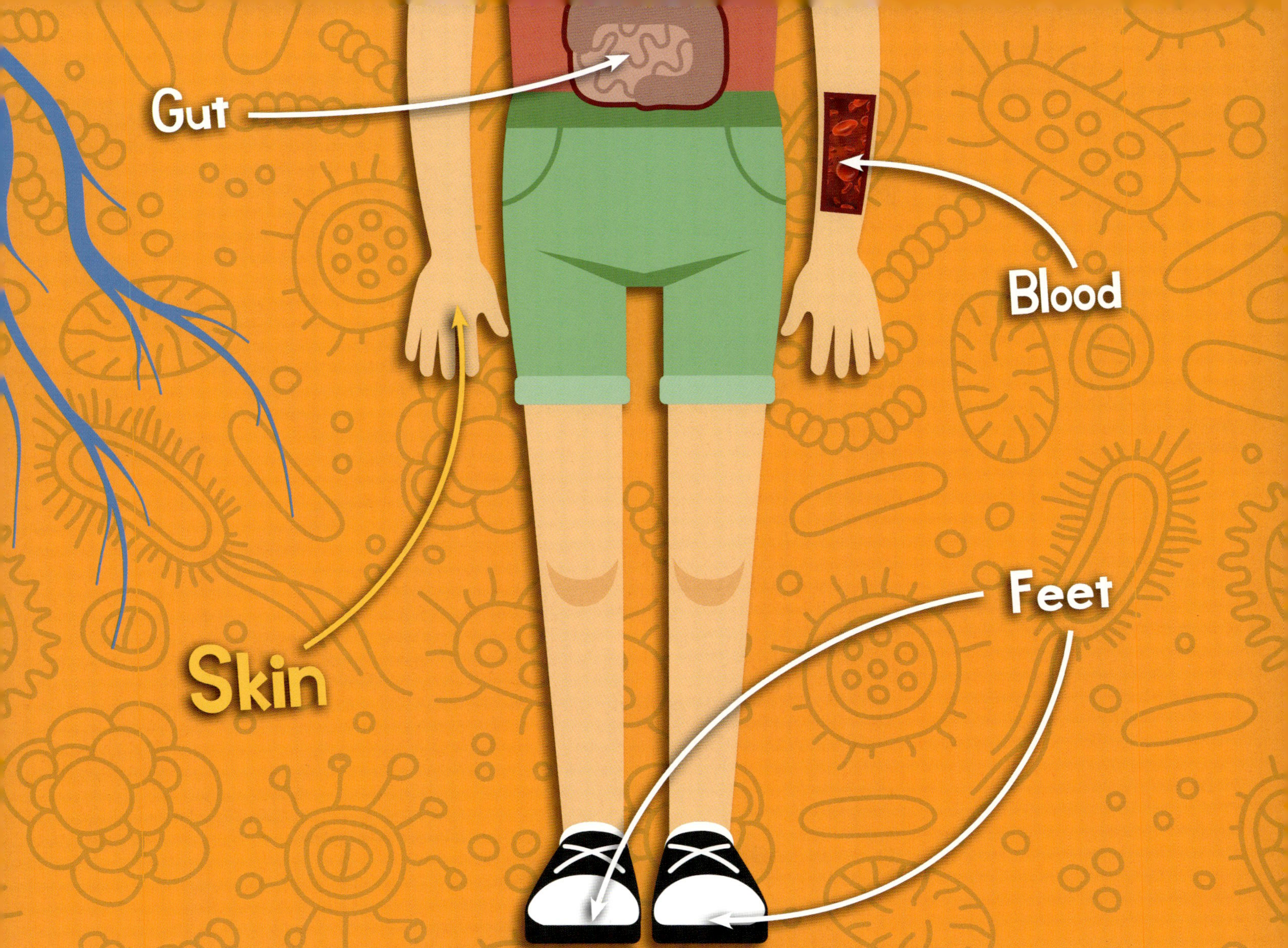

Just like planet Earth, with its different habitats and the different animals living in them, the human body has many different places that are home to lots of tiny living things. Today, we will be exploring the skin and just a few of the things living on it.

SENSATIONAL SKIN

Stretching from the forest of hair on the head all the way to the fungus-infested feet, skin covers the human habitat. But what lives on all those bits of skin in between?

Let's walk along the belly and see what we can find. There are bugs and bacteria all over the skin, but a lot of them are so small you can't see them.

UNWANTED VISITORS

The skin gets a lot of visitors. I think I see a bedbug over there. They don't live on the human habitat, but they visit to feed on the blood below the skin.

Oh, we are lucky, that is a body louse over there. They are a lot like bedbugs. They live in clothing and use their strong, hooked legs to hold on and drink blood.

ENTER THE BELLY BUTTON

The belly button is a great place for life to grow, especially in an innie! It is warm, damp, and there is lots to eat if you like dead skin and sweat.

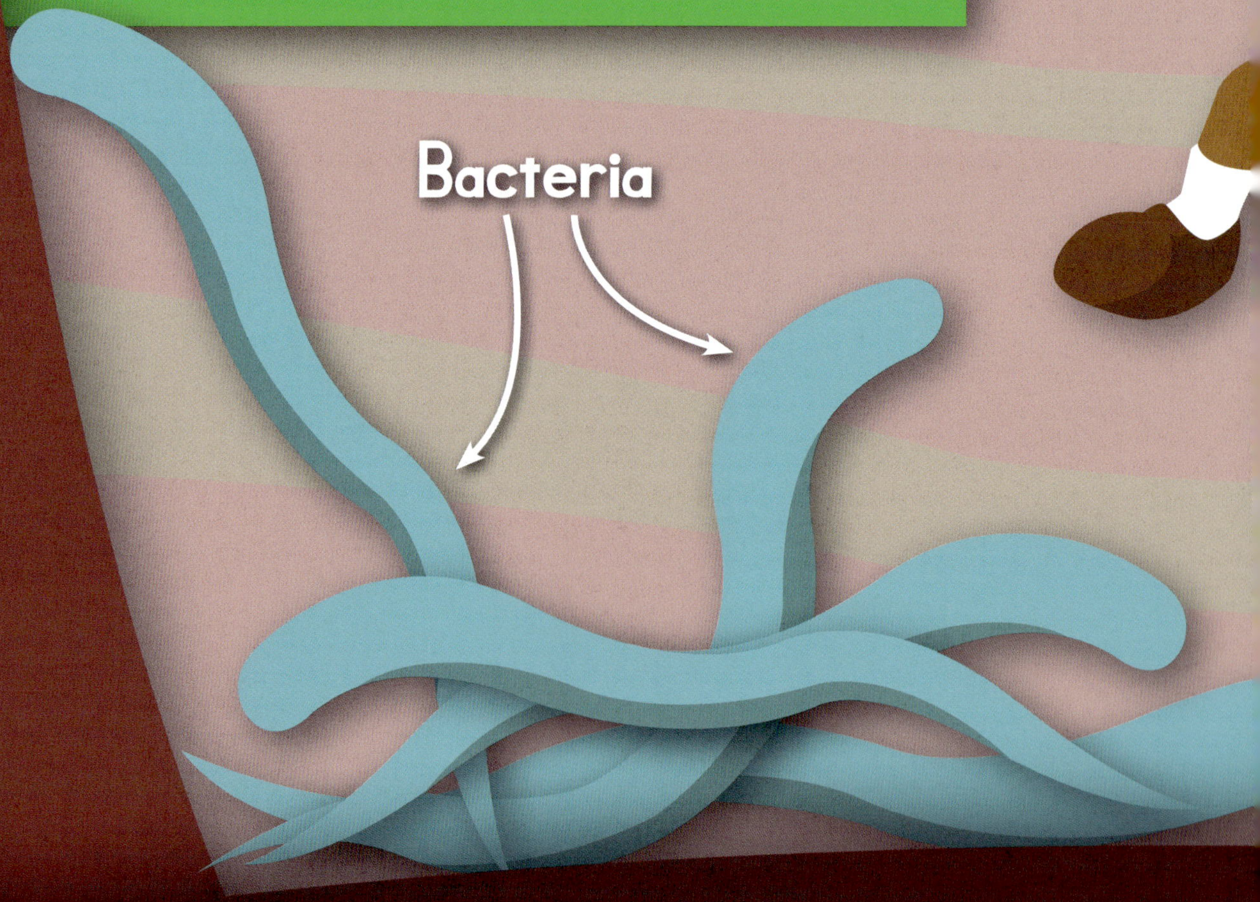

If those bacteria get enough food in there, they could really get out of hand. If that happens, this belly button could get very smelly.

PORES FOR THOUGHT

Can you see these tiny holes? They are pores. Special oils come out of the pores and spread over the skin. The oil is really good for it.

If those pores get blocked up with bacteria and oil, the habitat's defenses will close them off. This makes pimples. I'm just going to poke this one with a stick!

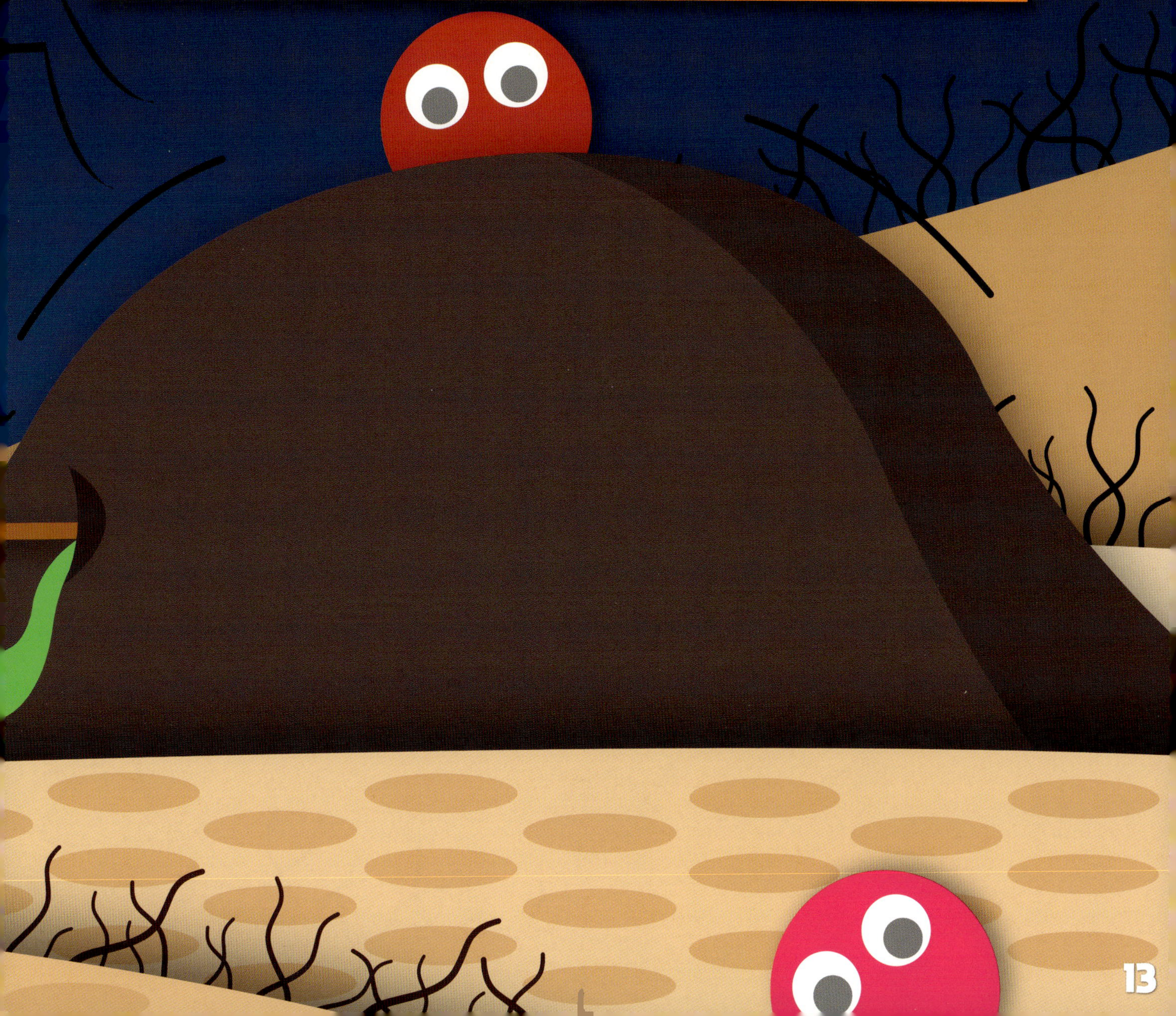

THE MITE-IEST OF ALL

Is that another pimple over there? No, wait. That isn't a normal pimple. Can you see the burrow under the skin? I think this is an infestation of scabies mites.

The female mite burrows under the skin to lay its eggs. This leaves a bump that looks like a pimple. We are really lucky to find one!

There are usually only 10 to 15 scabies mites on a human habitat at any one time.

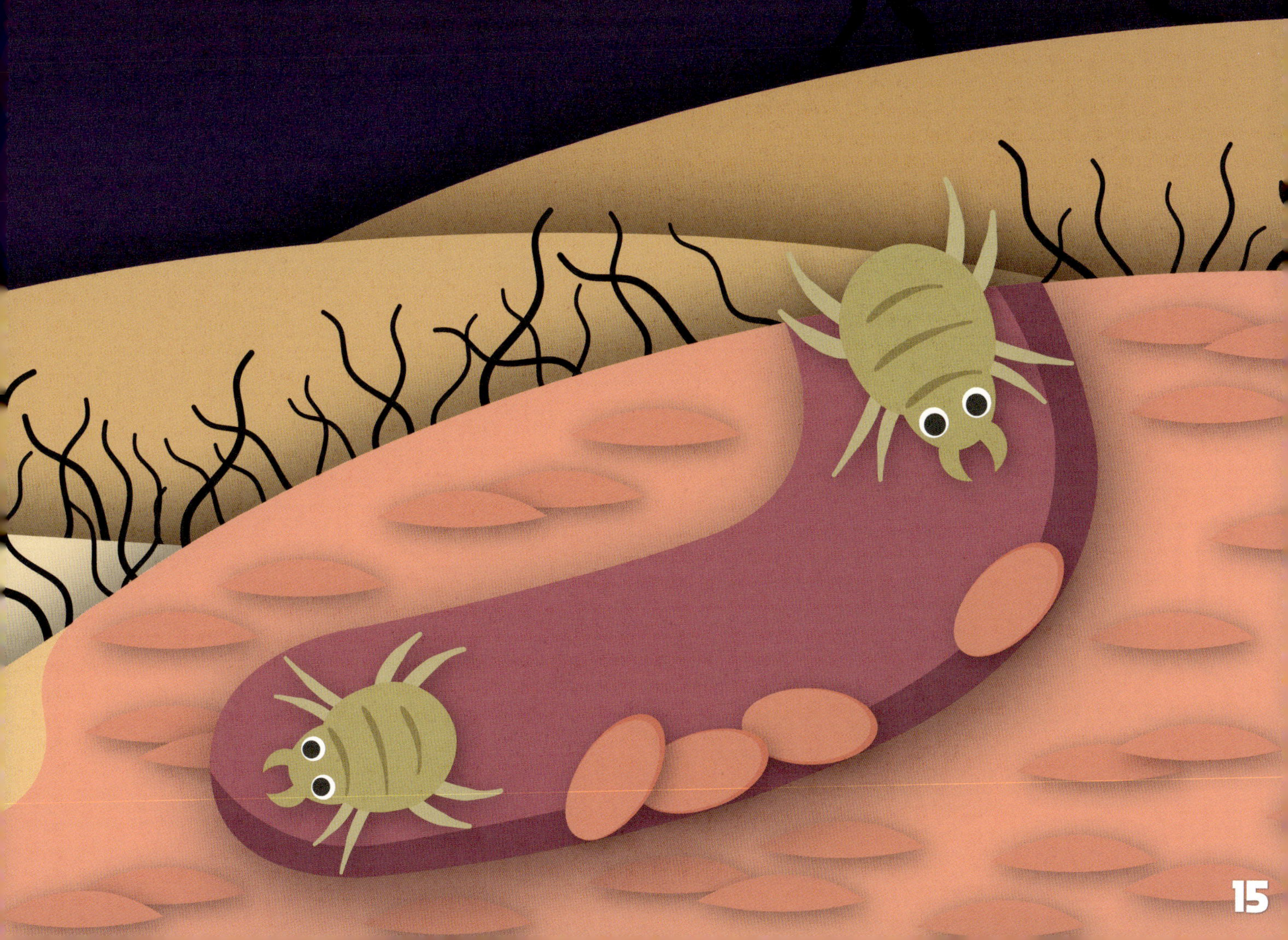

FREAKY FUNGI

Wow, look at this big red circle. That's ringworm! Don't worry, there isn't really a worm there. It is caused by a fungus, one that is a bit like the fungus that causes athlete's foot.

The fungus lives on top of the skin, where it eats keratin. Keratin is found in skin, hair, and nails. This fungus really likes to spread, so don't get too close!

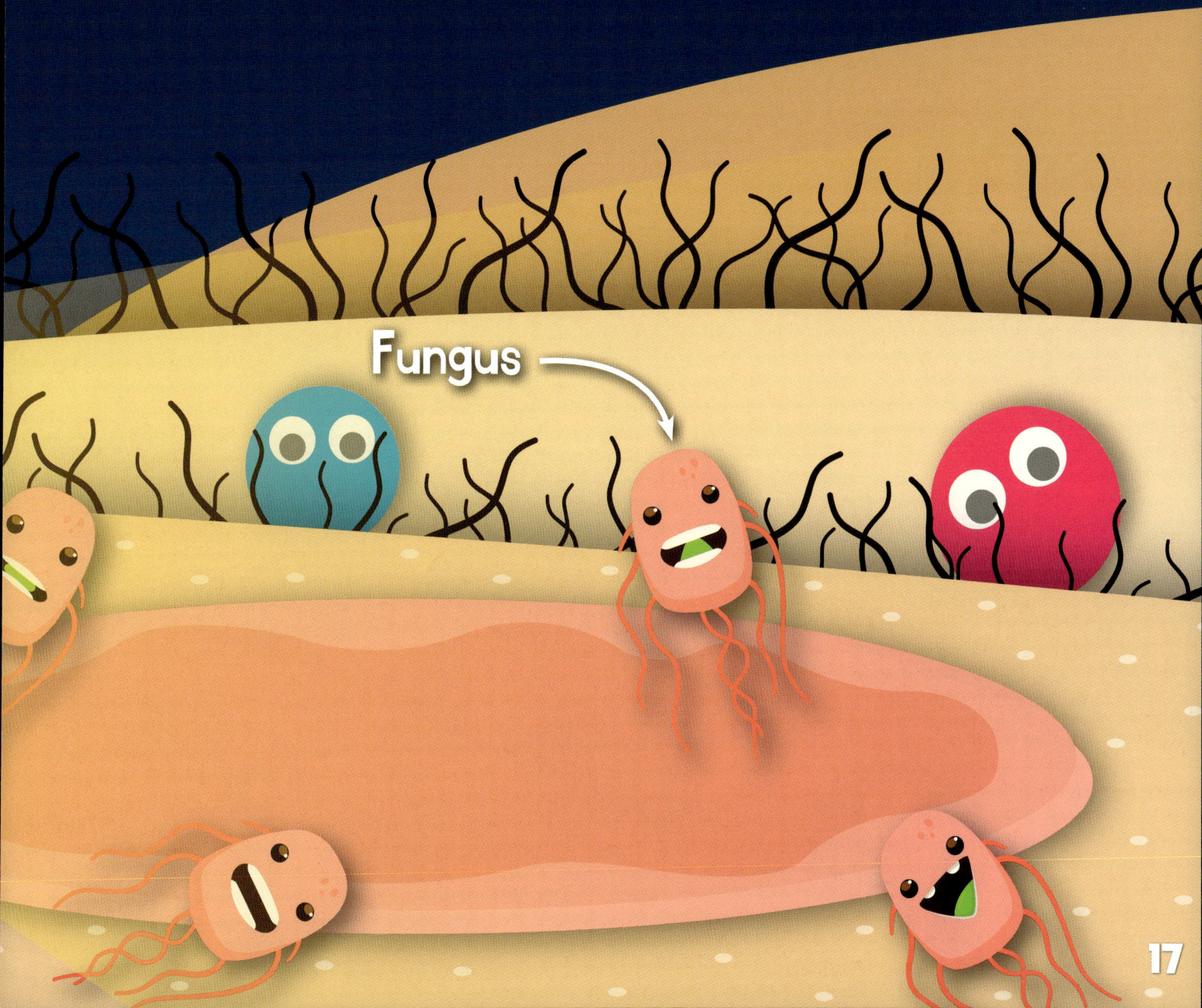

WARTS AND ALL

If we shimmy down the arm all the way to the hand, we will find something very special. No, that is not a tiny cauliflower. It is a palmar wart.

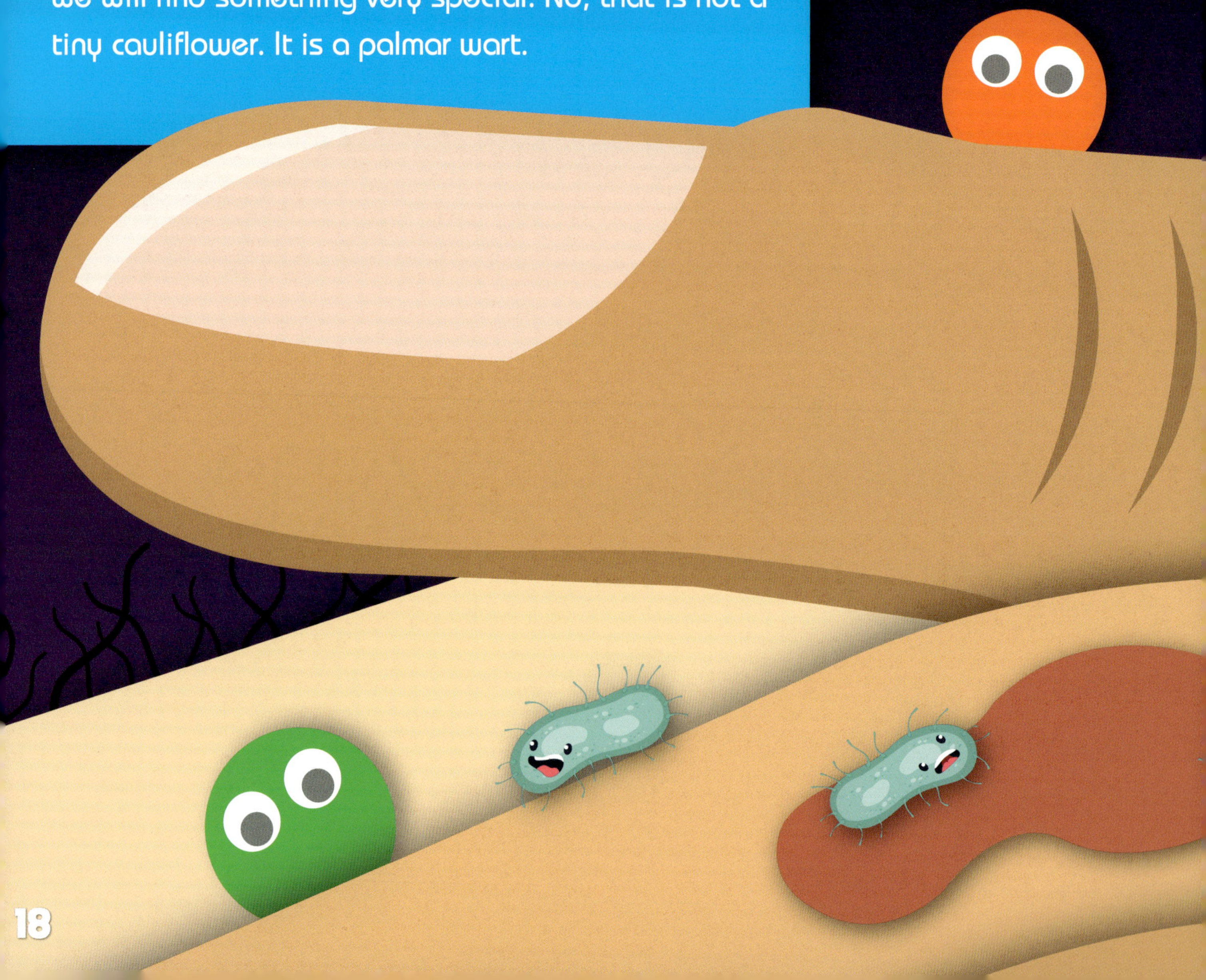

Warts are caused by viruses. Look, I think I see some by the wart now. They cause the skin to make more and more skin cells that become a wart.

SURPRISE PARASITE!

Wait, what is that rumbling? It feels like something moving under our feet. Oh look, you can see it tunneling. It must be a hookworm!

The hookworm will soon travel through the bloodstream to the lungs. After that, it will move to the gut and start making eggs.

MISTAKEN IDENTITY

Well, there was a lot of skin to cover, but I think we got to see most of it. Who would have thought that there would be so much life on the human habitat?

Hey, what's that up there in the sky? Is it a bird? Is it a plane? No, it's tweezers...
I think the habitat has mistaken me for a parasite. This is probably going to be the end of this adventure. See you soon.
Byeeeeeeee!

GLOSSARY

athlete's foot	a fungal infection of the foot
bacteria	tiny living things, too small to see, that can cause diseases
cells	the basic building blocks of all living things
defenses	things used for protection
documentary	a film that looks at real facts and events
habitat	the natural home in which animals, plants, and other living things live
infested	when germs, diseases, or other things from outside have entered part of the body
innie	a belly button that goes inward rather than sticking outward
mites	tiny arachnids of the same family as spiders
viruses	tiny living things that live inside other things and make them ill

INDEX